Terry Treetop and the Christmas Star

Written by Tali Carmi

Illustrated by Mindy Liang

Free gifts and free educational online games
are available on my website.

www.thekidsbooks.com

Enjoy!

Terry Treetop and the Lost Egg
Tali Carmi

Copyright © 2017 by Tali Carmi
All rights reserved. No part of this book may be used or reproduced in any manner whatsoever without the written and signed permission of the author, except in the case of brief quotations embodied in critical articles or review.

Translated to English by Taira Rider
Illustrations by Mindy Liang

Here are some of the ways to contact me:
Website: www.thekidsbooks.com
Twitter: tbcarmi
Facebook: Tali.Carmi.Author
LinkedIn: Tali Carmi
Join mailing list: www.thekidsbooks.com/join-mailing-list
mail: tcarmi@naharsite.com

ISBN 978-1979985826

Terry Treetop
and the Christmas Star

Written by Tali Carmi

It was Christmas Eve and the air smelled of cake,
People were skating on a big, frozen lake,
In windows, green and red lights were twinkling,
And all around you could hear small bells tinkling.

Mom was baking cookies, with flour in her hair,
Dad was hanging a garland around the door by the stairs.
Terry sat by the window with cocoa in his hand
Looking outside at the snow-covered land.

Outside, it had started heavily snowing
While in the hearth a warm fire was glowing.
The china laid out was the very best
Since they were expecting some wonderful guests.

Then Mom gave out a cry of panic so strong
That Terry and Dad turned to see what was wrong.
"I came out of the kitchen and what do I see?
We have not decorated our beautiful tree!"

"The guests are meant to arrive in an hour
And I am still all covered in flour!"
To their feet Terry and Dad quickly hopped,
Hanging the ornaments, from bottom to top.

All that was left was a bright, yellow star
When Dad said: "No, the top is too far.
I cannot reach it, I tried and I tried,
I'll have to get a ladder from the tree house outside."

Terry took his binoculars from the small shelf
To check if Dad could carry the ladder by himself.
He pointed it at the snow-covered tree
And in it, he surely had something to see!

He took his coat and followed his Dad through the snow
Which was up to his knees, so he went quite slow.
Terry yelled after him "Dad, can you see?
There's a frozen squirrel up in the tree!"

Dad rushed to help but the tree was too tall,
And he saw that the ladder was no good at all.
It started to creak just under his toe,
A small crack - and his foot was back in the snow.

"It's dangerous to climb, now what will we do?
Terry could see his Dad was worried too.
"Do not worry, Daddy, I will climb the tree,
It's not for nothing that I'm called Terry Treetop you see!"

Terry climbed to the treehouse, swift and fast-paced,
Knowing deep down they had no time to waste.
Taking the squirrel, he climbed down with alarm,
Scared he might cause the poor creature some harm.

They took it inside and wrapped it all snug,
In front of the fire, it was laid on the rug.
They put a hot water bottle right by its side
Everything they could think of that might help, they tried.

They were really quite worried 'bout a creature that size
But soon it slowly opened its big, black eyes.
They gave it some water, it wiggled its nose,
And in a moment or two, to its feet it rose.

"What happened?" Terry asked, "Are you okay?"
The squirrel took a big breath and began to say:
"My name is Sammy and it's my first winter,
And I have never been much of a sprinter.

When it got cold, to their dens squirrels ran,
But I did not make any sort of plan.
Your treehouse looked like a good place to hide,
I thought it would be a bit warmer inside."

Then the doorbell rang and Terry made a plea:
"Sammy, will you please help us finish our tree?"
With the star in his teeth, Sammy started to hop
And in a few seconds scurried straight to the top.

The star shone brightly from the top of the tree,
Overlooking the guests, all happy to see
Terry's new friend Sammy among the twigs,
Enjoying his dinner – his favorite – dried figs!

Thank you!

Thank you for purchasing this book!
You are most welcome to visit my website,
play free educational online games and download free gifts.

Enjoy!

www.thekidsbooks.com

More books in the **Terry Treetop** series

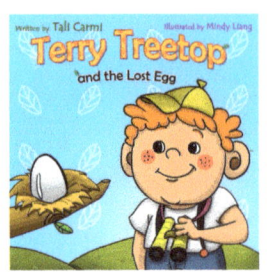 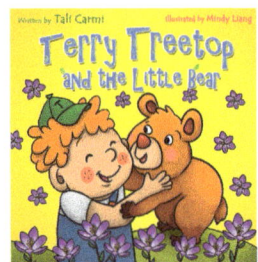 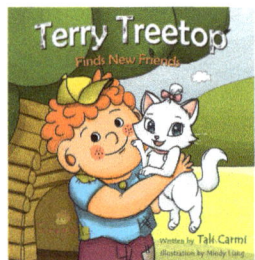 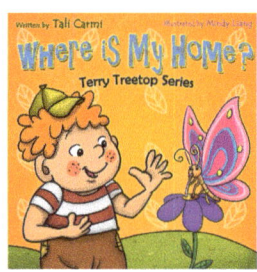 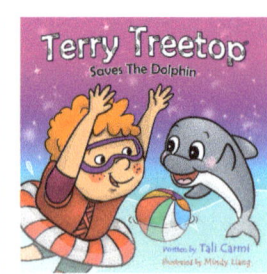

More books in the **Abigail** series

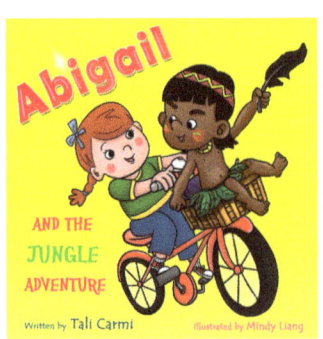 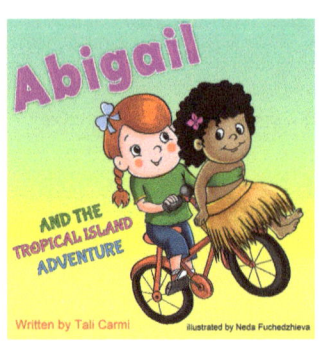